O POSITIVE

by the same author

fiction

SUBMARINE

WILD ABANDON

THE ADULTERANTS

JOE DUNTHORNE

O Positive

FABER & FABER

First published in 2019
by Faber & Faber Ltd
Bloomsbury House
74–77 Great Russell Street
London WC1B 3DA

Typeset by Hamish Ironside
Printed in the UK by TJ International Ltd, Padstow, Cornwall

A CIP record for this book is available from the British Library

ISBN 978–0–571–34255–6

2 4 6 8 10 9 7 5 3 1

For Maya

Acknowledgements

Thanks to the editors of the following publications where versions of these poems first appeared: *Poetry Wales*, *Poetry Review*, *Literary Review*, *Magma*, *New Statesman*, *London Review of Books*, *Granta*, *clinic*, *White Review* and *Five Dials*.

For reading and commenting on drafts of these poems, thanks to Rachael Allen, Emily Berry, Chris Hicks, Wayne Holloway-Smith, Luke Kennard, Kate Kilalea, Nick Laird, John Osborne, Holly Pester, Heather Phillipson, Sam Riviere, Ross Sutherland, Jack Underwood and Hannah Walker. Extra thanks to Sam for allowing me to use a phrase from his novel *Safe Mode*. Thanks to Peter Macneal for help with the surgical elements of 'Skilled labour'.

Thanks to Matthew Hollis, Lavinia Singer and everyone at Faber. Thanks to Georgia Garrett and everyone at RCW. Thanks to the Society of Authors for an Arthur Welton Award which bought me time to focus on this book. Love and thanks to Priya, Nicholas, Nisha, Tim, Kester, Anna, Marc, Luke, Leah, Katie, Mum, Dad – and specially to Maya and Lorne.

Contents

A

A sighting 7
I wanted to see how unhappy I could get 8
In which I practise happiness 9
Worship 10
Entertaining with hypnotism 11
I decided to stop therapy 12
At thirty-three I finally had the dream 13
Skilled labour 14
I finish my own sentences 15
Old days 16

B

Owls-in-law 19
Fizz 20
Good listener 21
Though the officer 22
How are you, coworker? 23
House guests 24
Promenade 25
Dinner 26
Dig 27
Sweetheart underwater 28

AB

The spins 31
Filters 32
Who killed these people? 34
All my friends regardless 35
Sestina for my friends 36
I am stupid with 38
In view of this retrospective it's easy to see that cubism began when I 39
Before you deplane 40
On crutches 41
Afternoon meditation at the ecovillage 42

O

Ransom tape 45
In the dream 46
My hostess and I, forever 47
Layers of Toine 48
Primary influences 49
Your lips are lovely by which 50
At last I am chosen 51
Workshop dream 52
Intelligent animals 53
After I have written my important poem 54

O POSITIVE

Always Open – Always Closed
– VAN KANNEL REVOLVING DOOR COMPANY

A

A sighting

As we waited to be torn apart
I remember thinking the bear
looked like an actor in a bear suit
who had quit his frontier theme park
to live in the hills, eat ear-frill fungus,
scratch his pelt on oaks cracked wide
by lightning and in time forget
his name and how to walk so that
when he found us pegging out
the groundsheet with absolute
devotion he sensed in each of us
a black bear beneath the Gore-Tex,
balancing well on our hind legs,
playing at language and marriage,
and his respect for our commitment
to character was why he did not
open us up.

I wanted to see how unhappy I could get

and it was very. I did not know
where I'd go to do it, somewhere not as
beautiful. My life was hopeless when
it was. I had the thinnest skin
since sliced. Then God in the shape
of a young professional paused
her soft commute. And she did recommend
a man who shut his eyes before he spoke.

And he never let my jokes
be jokes, never gave my pain
a prize. And in time I did step clear
of his unaffordable home to kneel
in a garden square that was open to non-residents
just this one day of the year. And there
I thought of other words for the little bitty sticks
of grass that were not leaves or blades.

In which I practise happiness

I love pigeons even
when their claws are stumps
and they walk as though in heels.
I love guinea pigs
for the idea they are in some way
a pig. Their heartbeats make their bodies
vibrate. I like to pretend
to answer them: 'whom may I say is speaking?'
I love football. More people love football
than love social justice
but that doesn't mean football
isn't brilliant. Whenever I head the ball
I feel a poem evaporate.
        I hate the bit of the poem
        where you're obliged
        to hate something.
I love the piano.
I love true crime.
I love the sun
when it arrives
like a tray of
drinks.

Worship

When picking your spot, look for a balance
of elements. Always show respect to those
wearing lower factors than you. Always check
downwind before shaking out your towel.

Lie back. Let the sand create a duplicate
of your spine. Match your breath to the tide.
Form not one opinion on the noises other
humans make. Let your body do the thinking.

On the backs of your eyelids, you will likely
see your childhood sweetheart in flames,
doused in lamp oil. This is natural.
Let them dance. You deepen by the hour.

Entertaining with hypnotism

'When I click my fingers,' I said, unaware of my mother
in the second row, her head lolling on her chest,
'you will be seventeen and in search of a dance partner.'
The guy she hauled up had forfeited depth perception
in pursuit of the perfect fringe; Iron Maiden
dog tags revealed his name as Richard. They moved
in most unlikely ways to imaginary reggae.

'Nine months go by and surprise, you have a child,'
I explained. Richard got shy and slunk back to his seat.
Mother called him a god-damn coward. The crowd
were on her side. I told her, 'Years pass and alone
you raise the child. He grows up talented, handsome . . .
a hypnotist. He makes anything you want to happen
happen.' She requested the power to mesmerise.

My mother was a natural, working the hall,
putting people under, saying 'When you wake
you will be transformed into hypnotists. All except you.'
We rounded on Richard. He said he was not suggestible
but she just swept aside his fringe to access both eyes
as we closed in with our full spectrum voice, speaking
in unison – 'you're irretrievably tired' – until his head dropped.

We decided that when we clicked our fingers
he'd wake in a loveless world and remain there for all time.

I decided to stop therapy

because I was perfect.
And how might your perfection
appear to others?
Classic my therapist,
missing the point completely.

At thirty-three I finally had the dream

where I made love to my mother.
I kept saying you are my mother
and she said I absolutely am.
Then she phoned my father
and told him everything.

Skilled labour

If you really love someone imagine a team of world-class plastic surgeons very delicately harvesting their face *en bloc* – hairline to neck – taking special care to preserve retention ligaments then expediting it, the face, by high-speed courier to the oak-bark tanners who cure it in formaldehyde, stretch it on a rack to the size of, let's say, a domestic trampoline, these dimensions precisely matched by the sculptor who builds up the chicken-wire armature replica of the loved one's skull and beautifully complex ears, using layers of dental plaster, gesso and a hessian scrim, before the face is glued back on, septum and eye slots trimmed, the surface groomed for the photorealistic painters' lash-thin brushes to accurately capture the three equidistant forehead wrinkles which resemble waves taking shape out at sea.

Jost Haas, last of the great ocularists, blows the eyes by hand, matches not just colour but the tributary veins of the sclera, captures the soul while resisting the urge to romanticise, after which wigmakers spritz strips of cotton lace, pin them to the scalp's perimeter before the bonded locks of a hundred strangers are sewn to the weft with a ventilating needle and only then is the whole structure winched atop a scaffold, set some way back in the garden, just far enough that the face appears the same size as the one across the table.

I finish my own sentences

I am in love with your wife but also in love
with the very idea of other people's wives.
And this hotel is full of them. I can hear
the lifts descending from the higher floors,
little boxes of happiness, hanging from a rope.

If I wait long enough all elevator doors peel back
on two lovers slathered in golden light, laughing
at a joke I did not catch, one reaching out to break
the sensor, the other easing a keycard from a clutch,
nodding as I take their place in the private dream

where I always find a pair of mes, coupled off
in mirrored walls, showing almost no
disgust before they both lean in.

Old days

Remember when everyone on earth
was pregnant except for you
which was a miracle

and the babies jangled down on their cords
like masks during sudden
cabin decompression

and all language was lost to the cutesy voice?
'Woo are so wucky,' everyone explained,
as you adopted

the brace position, amazed at the serenity
that comes from looking after
yourself.

B

Owls-in-law

These birds have no idea how to behave,
pouring glasses of water for just themselves,
regurgitating pellets of compressed bone
and now, landing on my daughter's arms.
As she laughs, their apertured eyelids click.
When she asks which of them are single
their lighthouse smiles sweep the room.

That night I watch my daughter sleep.
I'm at her bedside. They're in the eaves.
As she starts to dream, her eyes toil
in their sockets; I warn the owls not to
mistake this twitching for field mice
and pluck them out. I know from research
the power of their zygodactyl talons.

Their wings are silent when they descend,
claws now trimmed and tagged
with commitment rings. Her eyes stay shut
as they grip her clavicles, rising gently
between rafters. They hide in a darkness
to which my sight cannot adjust. I listen
for her cries but hear only deepening breath.

Fizz

Idiot balloonists
complicate our rear-view mirrors,
their flames changing colour
as they seek a height
at which the tiny little ant people
of which I am one
go about their ridiculous lives.

And though they do sometimes die,
balloonists,
most often they do not,
brought down by their ground crew
in cabbage fields.

Good listener

Be upset near me please, friends and colleagues, I am anxious that although you look happy you are not so let me hold your shoulders in the service lift until you speak your medicine – 'Cipralex, Cipralex, Cipralex' – and, like that, the doors slide back and we step out among acid-free box files, aware that we are inside it then, your pain, that this endowment-funded archive maintains your regrets in folio, and though we will feed the shredder, braid your hair with its ribbons, it can never be enough and you will need to burn this whole place down if only someone thoughtful has a light.

Though the officer

finds no bales of dope gaffered to my lumbar
the tender way he thumbs my waistband
suggests he is seeking other lives
that only my kind hips might defuse
the bar fights I see teeming in his eyes.

How are you, coworker?

‘I feel the same,’ I yell, loud as a drawer
of hotel cutlery, ‘exactly the same,’
my mouth so wide they can’t avoid
my fillings made of grey amalgam,
my feelings made of gold.

House guests

As a privilege
of my nearly hairless body
I invite ancient men to my bed.

We mostly top
tail but when we spoon
they keep their Great War coats on.

They whisper
about camp latrines, executions
at dawn, the stench beneath their bandages

and only perk up
when I interpret their dreams
which are always fiendishly literal.

Promenade

I was pursued by an immersive theatre troupe.
They stole my phone then rang my wife
who did not answer; an actor portrayed her mobile

vibrating towards the edge of a stranger's bedside table.
When she did call back they had changed my ringtone
to 'defibrillators'. An actress in a bib gripped my waist

and whispered 'tell her you never want to lose her'
then said it again in Portuguese before dying
unconvincingly in my arms. I told Maya

I was in a kitchen emporium but tried to embed it
with meaning. That ended the experience. I followed
the handsome actor who had played the phone

and asked if he made a living by acting because
I know it is tough. I followed him underground.
I was beginning to understand, I said, the underlying

power of the work. He said he was late to meet someone.
All the way home I eye-fucked the other people
on the train. They were all actors and actresses.

I asked them how they made a living.

Dinner

It is nice to imagine my significant other alone
forever with ravioli in the cafe where they know her name
but mispronounce it. I need to be realistic though
so I think of her in the Korean place she and her gay
colleagues frequent – tossing porterhouse on a hot plate
and taking compliments badly. To make life harder
for myself I then straighten one of the men. He dismantles
a raw egg salad and glistens at the lips. In time I turn
two more, to see how I handle it. Soon they're all enjoying
the raw egg salad. Next thing you know she asks
for her steak *bleu*. They've entered what looks
like a parlour. The waiter's not even Korean.

Dig

I saw Leonard once a month – no kissing, no nurse's uniform –
just specific pain in a midtown loft. We had no safe word
but I knew to stop if he reached for his inhaler.

He showed up at school as a whole body donor,
looking mellow on a gurney, just slightly
more unhealthy than when I last saw him alive.

Our tutor plucked his liver, his clouded heart, the lungs
shrunk to *pollo milanese*. When we moved to smaller blades
I raised my hand to volunteer. It was like old times,

just deeper. How he kept that melanoma to himself
I'll never know. I shaved it with a filament and suction hose.
We saved the head till last and – Leonard would have said

this was unimaginative – took the direct route in
with mallet, chisel, spreader. I was sad to see his tongue
without its barbell, no ash on its tip, but I was back

in the lounge of our suffering as I heard his eyeteeth chip.

Sweetheart underwater

Last thing I knew we were justifying the chlorine
in your parents' pool, the summer your kinder brother
came home late, a little drunk, and slept in the garden house
with the gas heaters on but unlit, and I don't remember

if you let me drift or I you, only that I still hold
the record, squinting up from the bottom of the deep end,
heart rate slowed to that of a baleen whale,
lungs burning, eyes on fire, watching the lot of you melt.

AB

The spins

This festive season I will murder myself or you,
either swing from the beams like the surume/
Bündnerfleisch/culatello of my native Japan/
Switzerland/Italy or hide beneath your bed
then hurt you. You kill me by which I mean
I like your jokes. In my country we open
our stomachs with a tantō/drink a glass
of pentobarbital/wade into the Adriatic.
I love you so much/it hurts/so much I love you.
You make me perfectly unhappy. We die
most nights but no relief. Call me Jun/Josef/
Giuseppe. I do hope I never see you again.
For the love of God, come home: it's the
emperor's birthday/Christmas/Santa Lucia.

Filters

My big sister rings to say she is riding around
on the back of Richard's motorbike
and would I like to meet for a drink.
Richard is a married man.
My sister is gay and I am always
dropping this into conversation.

Her ex-girlfriend says
that every bar should have non-male space
just like you have non-smoking.
She has a helmet under her arm
and a rum with ginger beer.
I used to ask my sister
if she had dismantled the patriarchal hegemony yet
which was a joke.

We're talking about marathon training.
The pub is beneath a brick railway bridge. The light
is greenish and you can feel the invisible trains.
Out front they're selling oysters on a school desk.
My sister says, 'How about it?'
When we were young we used to fight.
She chipped my tooth with a door stop.
I will eat anything.

The oysters smell of tin foil.
They are still alive.

My sister thinks I should chew a few times;
Richard says I should swallow it whole.
The creature is in my mouth
and now I must decide.

Who killed these people?

Alex did,
with his left-the-gas-on breath.
        It was not me it was Annette
        who does not sleep.
        Through her door each night
        I hear the tearing human flesh.
Eczema is stress-related.
It flares up when I hear
our neighbour blitzing
his victims, calling it juice.
        That's your toxins talking.
        The culprit is Patricia who
        formaldehydes her fingernails
        so they look like pretty claws.
Please. The childless couple
at number ten make elderberry jam.
I've seen it hang in muslin
like a freshly popped-out eye.
        Come, let's point the finger
        at whichever finger pointed first.
        Now who of you was sensitive
        to my sweetheart's gas-leak breath?

All my friends regardless

come to my garden and pretend to get along.
Please let me introduce the scientists. Yes,
he studies the behaviour of bees.
Friends from my childhood,
I do not think you stupid and boring.
Assistant editors, step away from the pond.
This man has written a dystopian
sci-fi novel; this man is an eco-carpenter.

I am on the roof, feeling so various,
astonished by my own width,
with water bombs in each hand.

Sestina for my friends

I know what my friends are thinking
because of the things they say:
'Joe, you are shiny and worthwhile and always
thinking of others.' I am not so great.
I could name at least five people who are better.
Here's one of my faults: I'm forever calculating

how to present myself in any given situation. Calculating
people give W. G. Sebald's *Rings of Saturn* as a gift, and think
that the person receiving the book will think better
of them. After reading it they will say:
'Joe – it was beautiful, I mean, he's like the great
gramps I never had. He even made Suffolk compelling.' I always

give *Rings of Saturn* as a gift, sometimes even to boys. Always
is too much. I have given it twice, if I'm calculating
honestly. Once to a girl who thought I was great
for just over a month until she suspected, correctly, that I think
I am more interesting than her. If I say
that the boy I gave it to was better

at football than me then I think you understand. Better
to be left for dead on the right wing, always
knowing that the boy who embarrassed you – let's say
his name is Luke – has this book in his bedroom. I'm calculating
that he won't have sold it because he thinks,
nay *hopes*, that one day he might read it, this great

and clever book that was a gift from a friend who is not great
at football but by God he's got a brain and ultimately it's better
to have enormous thoughts than to be almost semi-pro. I think
great people do not have these kinds of thoughts. I always
keep my mauled copy somewhere half-inconspicuous,
    calculating
a spot where guests will see it, sure, but will not say

'I bet Joe put that there so I see it.' More likely they'll say
'Huh! Such a clever book just lying there next to his football
    boots. It is great
to know someone like Joe who is clever but doesn't rub your
    face in it. Calculating
people are the worst in existence.' This poem is better
for its honesty. Even when I admit all this stuff my friends can
    always
fall back on my honesty. He thinks

too much, they think. We had best not say
anything about that sestina. He'll always be great
to us, better than great, more like excellent. Or this is what I'm
    calculating.

I am stupid with

feelings, holding a red rose
like a tiki torch with which
to burn down the village
where everyone who isn't
the person I love lives.

In view of this retrospective it's easy to see
that cubism began when I

channelled the pure language of light and space and yet
I would have hated this statue, this memorial hiking trail
around (my adopted home) Lake Como, this sculpture
of dented lenses mending reflections of water to show how
I gave each object its soul, a word I rejected, of course.[1]

1 Along with all the other words, in my usual insouciant way.

Before you deplane

In our culture, it is frowned upon to carry your sadness like a tiny dog. In our culture, it is traditional to shop your neighbours for whoring and fraud. Actual tiny dogs we have time for, sweating from their stamp-sized tongues. They help us send the letters of condolence. We take no pleasure in our city breaks out of respect for the deceased. Our children are full grown by which we mean abroad.

In our culture, transplant organs come only from countries with a surplus. It is considered good luck if a medical courier overtakes. We memorise drunk drivers' plates through the medium of song. We tell the police everything about our home life. Here we have a saying: He who videos his neighbour's house fire will have no one with whom to share it. Our prisons fill with Daniels but still we love the name.

On crutches

Are you trying to say
you never leapt from a spinny chair
into the backing singers' arms
at the cutthroat barber's soft launch
yelling 'for I am the centrifuge,
all densities find kin within me' at which point
they all – ha! – totally caught you,
sang a melancholy chanson
to your charming, harmless mole
then later, as dawn repainted the playpark,
you shoulder-rolled in dismount
from the tyre's ecliptic swing – shoeless,
by now, you maniac – coming down
weird and hard on your ankle which shivered
but did not crack – ha! – ha! – and so
in fact I have no fucking idea
how you hurt yourself – probably in the shower –
you horrid, impossible man.

Afternoon meditation at the ecovillage

The focaliser's eyes pace back and forth
behind their lids. He inhabits his mind.
My stairwell's blocked with half-unpacked boxes.
One is labelled *my version of events* and rattles
when I shake it. I hear his throat creak
as the fifth dimension swings open.

What's he doing up there? How long
since he took the batteries out of the wall clock?
There's a knock at the tangible door.
Pottery's got the room from six.
Lucky for me I never found the inner attic.
Our diesel *Om* evokes a refuse freighter

pushing clear of the dock and – *like that* –
I'm among the gulls following its hump of landfill.
I realise I am *inside* myself, circling my innards.
One of the gulls says: 'Joe, our time is up.'
How true. My mind is alternately half empty,
half full at the sheer waste/dinner of it all.

O

Ransom tape

A boom or some fruit keeps bobbing into frame.
Our children are dressed in tracksuits the colour of aubergines.
They kneel in a clearing of sawgrass somewhere between
the equator and the Tropic of Capricorn. It feels wrong to say
the production values reassure us. At the press conference,
we make it clear we will not pay.
                                                            We pay,
handing a holdall to young men in Wendy's, Caracas,
while our kids, wrists tied, wait politely
in the accessible restroom; it unlocks from both sides.

In the dream

you had no talent
for folding parachute silks
but so endearing was your self-belief
we dared not spoil the feeling. Even those
in chutes that failed felt valued
as they fell.

Setting the general free
from his hair, nails and bridgework
felt so good you took scissors to the skin
below his ribs, a slit the width
of a child's fist then invited
little Ian in.

The general swore
to hunt you down in hell
which made you smile since you resisted
all god-terms and had no need of the comfort
promised by a secondary realm
which went without saying

in the dream.

My hostess and I, forever

Her boss nods
at us
as if
to say
our love
is too conspicuous.

That even when
she tongs
the ice
he sees
how much
she means it.

That I should buy
at least
another
foreign
spritz
to be polite.

That to flaunt
a love
this true
is cruel
to all
the regulars.

Layers of Toine

According to the Flemish psychoanalyst Toine Duijsens, there are five layers of self. The first, *the carapace*, in which we spend most of our lives, is a shell of acceptable attributes – friendliness, cruelty, wit, commitment – which the second layer, *the mirror*, reveals to us as a sham. That this feels like profound insight is practical because most of us will seek no deeper access. Layer three, *the river*, a necessarily pretty obstacle, is familiar to practitioners of meditation for whom the mind may clear a moment with a mellow epiphany – 'I think I see it moving, it's beautiful, so fast' – but who rarely move to cross it. If the mind does reach *the cavern* then the simple realisation that there is all this extra space falling away into darkness provokes an emotional/spiritual black-out sufficiently satisfying that it will pacify any ambitions to reach the final layer which Duijsens elected neither to name nor describe because he felt it would harm us too much to learn that our arrogance and blindness are perfectly balanced, that the meaning of life is how best to stop searching, a productive contradiction at the heart of his studies, ruining the trick by learning how it's done.

Primary influences

Before we had books
we had stories
and before stories
gossip and before gossip
private thoughts
about the ethics
of our neighbours
and before private thoughts
dreams of something
breathing in the grasslands
of our childhood
and before dreams
we kept our sleep thin
to hear the hacksaw pant
of the shape as it ate
a neighbour or
a stranger
if a neighbour
we carved
an eye
to guard
where we slept
if a stranger
we marvelled
at the pattern
of their struggle
in the dirt
then took turns saying
what it looked like.

Your lips are lovely by which

I mean love me by which I mean
babies, big ones. Let's have ones
that laugh even though they
cannot walk. Let's have one
a month. I think I'm finally ready.

At last I am chosen

for extended security. The man passes his wand
across my groin. Wow, the wand says, wow.
That's my soul, I explain, as he pulls wide
my buttocks, admires the tuft of
cling film, a small pale flame.

Workshop dream

All poets lived in one low-rise resort.
Sleepwalking, I climbed across white balconies
to Sean O'Brien's split-level apartment.
I expected him to be angry but he wasn't.
He said I was not the first poet to arrive
this way. Inside, Koch was cooking breakfast,
a Faber editor was applying after-sun
and there was a woman I'd not read.

We walked through the quadrant
in O'Brien's slipstream, noticing everything
worth noticing: the blanched undersides
of leaves, George Szirtes's towel,
the memory of wet feet on stone.

We stepped onto the beach. The water
made the sound: cliché, cliché, cliché.
We shooed away the avant-garde
who sold necklaces made from shattered
windscreen glass. 'Tiny grains of sand,'
I added. Sean, our windbreak, shook his head
and pointed out to sea but there was nothing.
He advised us to look again and this time,
sure enough, on the surface in the troughs
between waves: a huge flock of addenda.

Intelligent animals

The pigs are happy
and we cannot understand why.
We mention heavy industry
but they shrug and make a contented sound
from deep inside their rectangular bodies.
What about the press, we say,
where a pink man is worth fifty yellow ones?
They nuzzle the dirt and do a roly-poly.

We show them buckets of antiseptic.
We show them photos of cows on fire.
We show them a documentary
about intensive pig farming.

After I have written my important poem

I will write one about skiing
because where are the decent skiing poems
and some light verse for my friend's brother's civil ceremony
(even though I do not much like my friend's brother
but you can't say no to these things)
then a long one about *jambes lourdes* (heavy legs)
a condition from which only French people suffer
and though the poem may start as satire
it will slowly attain a terrible empathy
. . . *for are we not all girdered to every floor* . . . et cetera
the reader suddenly pinned to their seat
with compassion for the hypochondriac French
(despite the billion euros they waste each year
on special creams) and the poem will say surely
if we can understand I mean truly feel
the imagined heft of their legs
then we can love one another absolutely
which the reader will buy into (their critical faculties
by this point hopelessly diminished)
leaving me free to turn the poem's final lines
to Buzz Aldrin on the surface of the moon
released from the limbs
that bind us to the earth – Buzz Aldrin
running like how we run
in dreams

but first.